What Can You Do with a Tube?

by Gillespie Katt
illustrations by Susan Gal

Harcourt Brace & Company

Orlando Atlanta Austin Boston San Francisco Chicago Dallas New York Toronto London

"What can you do with a tube?" asked Mrs. Jules.

"What can you use it for?"

"I can use it with a cube!"
said Meg.

"I can strum it like a uke!"
said Zack.

"I can use it to make
something cute," said Kent.

"I can use it to make a mule," said June.

"I can use it as a wand,"
said Lin.

"I can use it to make a leg,"
said Jamal.

"I can use it as a bat,"
said Evan.

"You DO know what to do with a tube," said Mrs. Jules.

"When it's in this room with you and me, a tube can be what we want it to be!"